Contents

Chatty chimpanzees. 4

A chimpanzee's body 8

Life in Africa. 14

Growing up 24

Saving chimpanzees 28

Glossary 30

Books 31

Websites 31

Comprehension questions. 31

Index. 32

Chatty chimpanzees

A chimpanzee swings from branch to branch. It climbs down and hugs a friend. Then the chimps dig through each other's fur. They pick out insects and dirt.

Touch is an important way for chimpanzees to communicate. They groom and kiss each other. They hug and tickle.

5

Chimpanzees "talk" to each other in many ways. These primates scream, bark, yell and laugh. They chase each other and make faces. Chimpanzees do not hide their feelings. They are social animals that need to spend time with other chimps.

A chimpanzee's body

Chimpanzees belong to the ape family. Gorillas, orang-utans and humans are also apes.

Adult chimpanzees grow to 1.7 metres (5.5 feet) tall. They weigh up to 68 kilograms (150 pounds). Male chimps are larger than females.

A chimpanzee's face looks a lot like a human's. Chimps have small noses and eyes that face forwards. Like us, they can see in colour. Sight is their most important sense.

Brown or black hair covers a chimpanzee's body. Like humans, their hair goes grey as they age. A chimp may puff up its hair when angry or scared.

A chimpanzee's arms are longer than its legs. Chimps are called knuckle-walkers because they walk on all fours. They walk on two legs over short distances.

Chimpanzees have opposable thumbs and big toes. Their thumbs and toes make it possible for chimps to grip objects and swing from branches.

Life in Africa

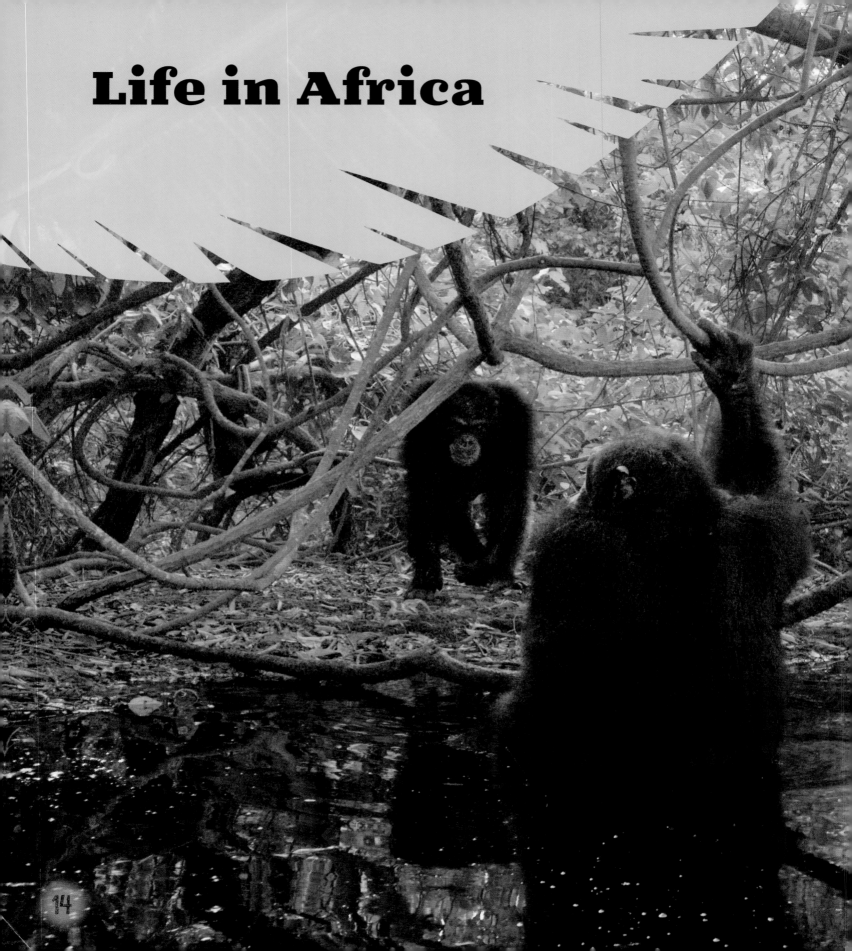

All wild chimpanzees live in Africa. Most are found in central Africa. Because chimps eat many types of food, they can live in different habitats. They are found in both rainforests and savannahs.

Africa

Where Chimpanzees Live

15

Chimpanzees live in groups called communities. Each community has between 15 and 120 chimps. One male leads each community. Chimpanzees eat, sleep and travel in smaller groups of about six chimps.

Sometimes the entire community
gathers together. The chimpanzees
play and groom one another.
It's like a party for chimps!

Chimpanzees spend most of their days eating and looking for food. They eat fruit, nuts, seeds, leaves, insects and small animals. They walk along the forest floor and climb trees. When one chimp finds food, it lets out a loud call. Other chimps come to enjoy the feast.

Do you use a fork or spoon when you eat?
Chimpanzees also use tools at mealtimes.
They break open nuts with rocks. They scoop
water from hollow trees using leaves.

Chimps "fish" for termites and ants by poking sticks into their nests. Then they pull out the sticks and lick off the insects. They even use leaves for napkins!

21

At night chimpanzees snooze in trees. They build nests of twigs and branches. Most nests sit at least 4.6 metres (15 feet) above the ground. Chimpanzees make new nests each night.

Each chimp sleeps in its own nest. They rest
their heads on pillows made from soft leaves.

Growing up

Female chimpanzees give birth to a single baby after about eight months. Baby chimps are called infants. At birth, infants weigh about 1.8 kilograms (4 pounds). They have light-coloured faces and a small patch of white hair on their rumps.

Female chimpanzees and their young have strong bonds. Infants hitch a ride on their mothers' backs for about two years. Mothers groom their young. They teach them how to crack open nuts and build nests.

Young chimps live with their mothers for six to nine years. But they remain close for life. In the wild, chimpanzees can live for up to 45 years.

Saving chimpanzees

Today chimpanzees are endangered. When rainforests are cut down, chimps lose their homes. They are hunted and even sold as pets.

Scientists such as Dr Jane Goodall have spent years studying chimpanzees. They set aside land for chimps to live on. Local farmers save rainforests by learning new ways to farm. Together they work to save these awesome animals.

29

Glossary

ape large primate with no tail; gorillas, orang-utans and chimpanzees are types of ape

bond feeling close to someone

communicate pass along thoughts, feelings or information

community population of chimpanzees living together in the same area and depending on each other

endangered in danger of dying out

groom to clean or make an animal look clean

habitat natural place and conditions in which a plant or animal lives

opposable able to be placed against one or more of the other fingers or toes on the same hand or foot

primate any member of the group of intelligent animals that includes humans, apes and monkeys

rainforest thick forest where a great deal of rain falls

savannah flat, grassy area of land with some trees

sense one of the powers a living being uses to learn about its surroundings; sight, hearing, touch, taste, and smell are the five senses

social living in groups or packs

Books

Endangered Animals (Eyewitness), Dorling Kindersley (Dorling Kindersley, 2010)

Animals in Danger in Africa Richard and Louise Spilsbury (Raintree, 2013)

Websites

http://kids.nationalgeographic.com/content/kids/en_US/ animals/chimpanzee/
Is a chimpanzee taller than a bus? Find this answer and more!

www.monkeyworld.org/userfiles/Banana%20Hunt.pdf
Help the chimpanzees through the maze to find the fruit!

Comprehension questions

1. Look at the pictures on pages 20–21. Describe how the chimpanzees' use of tools is similar to a human's.

2. On page 22, the text says chimpanzees make their nests at least 4.6 metres off the ground. Why don't they build their nests on the ground?

3. How do chimpanzees communicate? Explain how each form of communication might be useful to a chimpanzee community.

Index

colours 11, 25

communication 5, 6

communities 16, 17

food 15, 18, 20, 21, 26

grooming 4, 5, 17, 26

habitat 15

hair 11

infants 25, 26, 27

life span 27

nests 22, 23, 26

nose 10

sight 10

size 9

sounds 6, 18

tools 20, 21

walking 12